LET'S VISIT AUSTRIA

Let's visit
AUSTRIA

DEDICATION

For my nephew, Ian

ACKNOWLEDGEMENTS

The Author and Publishers are grateful to the following organizations and individuals for permission to reproduce copyright photographs in this book:

The Austrian Institute; the Austrian National Tourist Office; International Photobank; Eugenie Peter; Tony Stone Photolibrary – London.

In addition, the Author is grateful to Joan Todd for preparing the map, to A. Jennewein of the Austrian National Tourist Office, Dr. Bernhard Stillfriend, Director of the Austrian Cultural Institute in London and Dr. G. Schramel and the office of the Austrian Trade Commissioner, as well as to Andrew Codd and Nicholas Downing for technical assistance, Anthony and Walki Hall for their comments on the typescript, and the Anglo-Austrian Society for first introducing him to the land of the Austrians, more than twenty years ago.

The cover photograph of Tyrolean bandsmen is reproduced by permission of Peter Baker.

CIP data
James, Alan, 1943 *Aug.* 22 –
  Let's visit Austria
  (1.) Austria – Social life and customs – Juvenile literature
  I. Title
  943.6'053   DB27
ISBN 0 222 00940 3

Burke Publishing Company Limited
Pegasus House, 116–120 Golden Lane, London EC1Y 0TL, England.
Burke Publishing (Canada) Limited
Registered Office: 20 Queen Street West, Suite 3000, Box 30, Toronto, Canada M5H 1V5.
Burke Publishing Company Inc.
Registered Office: 333 State Street, PO Box 1740, Bridgeport, Connecticut 06601, U.S.A.
Typeset in "Monophoto" Baskerville by Green Gates Studios Ltd., Hull, England.
Printed in Singapore by Tien Wah Press (Pte.) Ltd.

Contents

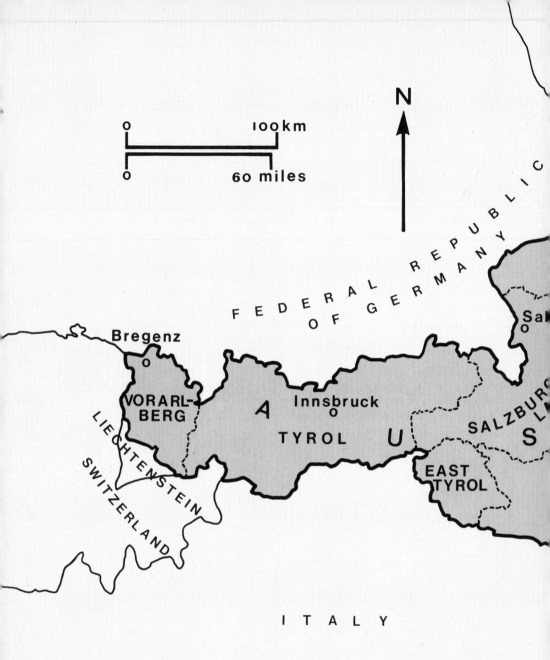

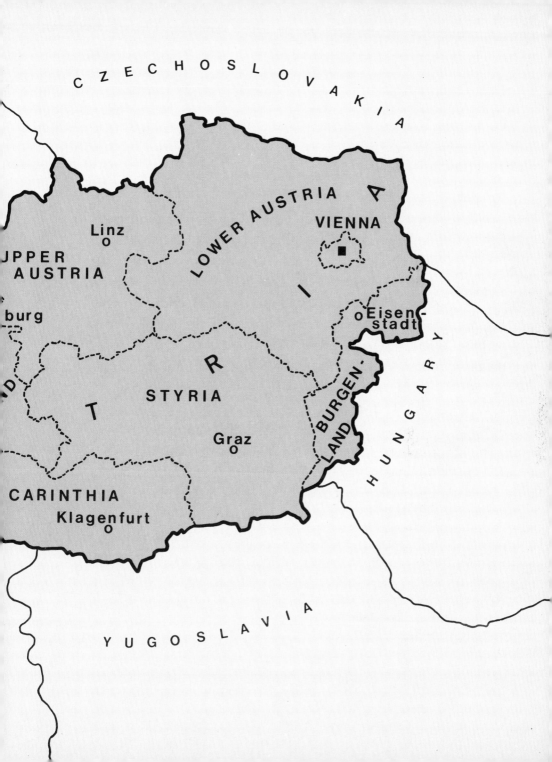

Introducing Austria

Austria is situated in the southern part of central Europe. It is a land-locked country (with no sea coast), surrounded by seven other countries (West Germany and Czechoslovakia to the north, Hungary to the east, Yugoslavia and Italy to the south and Switzerland and Liechtenstein to the west). Austria forms a large part of the eastern alpine region of central Europe.

The Alps are a huge mountain range 1,000 kilometres (620 miles) long, separating Italy from the rest of Europe. The central part of the range is in Switzerland but the mountains reach as far as France in the west and Austria and Yugoslavia in the east.

About three-quarters of Austria is mountainous—the highest mountain, the Grossglockner in the south, reaches 3,798 metres (12,461 feet). The limestone mountains in the north extend towards the Bavarian Alps in Germany. Close to the border with Italy are the Carnic Alps, while the Oetztal Alps are near Innsbruck, the Karawanken Alps are on the border with Yugoslavia and the Silvretta range border Switzerland. Long tunnels, such as the Tauern Tunnel, have been blasted through these mountains and impressive mountain roads, such as the Grossglockner Highway, have also been constructed.

Austria's scenery is extremely varied — this picture shows a pine forest with Mt. Dachstein (in the Alps) in the background

Austria is a land of beauty and contrasts. It has magnificent mountain scenery, beautiful cities with baroque architecture, quaint and attractive villages, impressive castles, forests and plains. The total area of Austria is 83,850 square kilometres (32,376 square miles)—about the same size as Ireland. The shape of the country is rather like a long pear on its side, with its stalk pointing westwards. Its population totals approximately 7,500,000.

Austria is at the centre of the European continent and her rivers, which flow in different directions to neighbouring countries, end in a number of seas. The River Danube rises in Germany, flows eastwards through Austria and then on to

The picturesque town of Hallstatt, on the shores of Lake Hallstatt in Upper Austria

Hungary, ending up in Romania and the Black Sea. The Inn flows to the Rhine, then into Lake Constance (a small part of which belongs to Austria) and ends up in the North Sea.

The Austrian climate is bracing and healthy but varies from region to region depending on the height of the surrounding mountains and the degree of exposure to northerly or southerly winds. In the mountains the air is clean and dry. The hills close to the Alps have the heaviest rainfall—more than 200 centimetres (80 inches) a year. The region east of Lake Neusiedl is much drier with a total annual precipitation (rain and snow) of less than 60 centimetres (24 inches).

Summers are warm and winters are cold. The average July midday temperature in Vienna is 24° Centigrade (75°

Fahrenheit), and in Salzburg 18° Centigrade (64° Fahrenheit). In winter, average temperatures fall as low as —2° Centigrade (28° Fahrenheit). In general, snow tends to fall on high ground and as the whole of Austria is more than 300 metres (1,000 feet) above sea level, snowfalls are common throughout the country. The amount of snow varies—Vienna averages 15 centimetres (6 inches), Innsbruck 30 centimetres (12 inches) and Seefeld 1.3 metres (50 inches).

Austria is one of the most heavily-forested countries in Europe. Oak and beech are common at low altitudes. On higher land, above 500 metres (about 1,600 feet) the oak gives way to fir. On even higher ground the fir gives way to

The River Danube flows east through Austria, passing many small villages such as this one

larch and stone-pine, and on the highest land of all trees do not grow as it is too cold.

In the foothills of the Alps there are large tracts of arable land and, especially on the northern edge of the Alps, there are grasslands.

The wildlife is typical of central European countries. It includes red deer, roe deer, wild boar, moufflon (wild mountain sheep), hare, fox, squirrel, pheasant and partridge and, in the higher mountains, chamois, marmot, Alpine hare, ptarmigan and ibex. In the reed-beds surrounding Lake Neusiedl there are purple heron, spoonbill and avocet.

A typical Austrian house in the snow-covered countryside

A wild boar with its young. This animal is a familiar sight in Austrian woods and forests

In the mountains of Tyrol, Carinthia and Vorarlberg many varieties of wild flowers bloom during the spring and summer, including the spring crocus, gentian (a deep blue mountain flower), orchid and mountain rhododendron. Here, too, such fruit as wild strawberry, raspberry, cranberry and bilberry are often found.

The Provinces of Austria

Austria is a federal state consisting of nine provinces: Vorarlberg, Tyrol, Salzburg Land, Carinthia, Styria, Upper Austria, Lower Austria, Vienna and Burgenland.

These provinces are like small countries within Austria and an Austrian owes allegiance to both his country and his province. Each province has a Governor who is elected by the provincial parliament. These Governors have much the same functions in their own provinces as the Federal Chancellor has in the government of the whole country. The members of the provincial parliaments are elected by ballot. The voting system is called proportional representation—which means that the number of seats which a party holds depends on the actual number of votes cast for that party. Each province decides how it should be run, so laws and even taxes vary from province to province. The provinces are divided into smaller units called districts. Each district has a local governor who is a civil servant—he is appointed rather than elected. Villages and towns have elected councils led by mayors and these councils concern themselves with local matters.

Each of Austria's nine provinces has its own distinctive culture, character and traditions. The qualities which make each province unique have evolved from differences in geography, climate and history.

VORARLBERG

Vorarlberg, in the west of Austria, is a small province where the people speak a dialect of German which is more closely related to the German spoken in Switzerland, over the border, than to that spoken in the rest of Austria. Its capital is Bregenz, on Lake Constance. The scenery here attracts many visitors, including those interested in alpine skiing. Others fish, sail and climb in summer.

Some Austrians in this part of the country find employment in catering for the needs of tourists, some in agriculture and others in industries such as textiles or paper production. Engineers have built huge hydro-electric power-plants to

The dam of an Austrian hydro-electric power plant

transform the pressure of the water from the rivers in the mountains into electricity. Power cables carry it for vast distances to provide heat and light in homes or power for industry. Some electric power is exported to neighbouring countries, such as West Germany.

Even the industrial towns of the region where textiles are manufactured are attractive places. Industrial plants have been built in such a way as to be unobtrusive in such towns as Dornbirn and Feldkirch. They are sometimes surrounded by picturesque streets, old inns and examples of the traditional crafts of woodcarving and wrought-iron work.

The province of Vorarlberg is in a rather isolated position. To the south are the mountains separating Austria from Switzerland; to the east are the mountains of Tyrol; and so travellers must journey over the Arlberg Pass or through the mountains by rail- or road-tunnel to reach it. It takes a train about seven minutes to travel through the Arlberg Tunnel. In the north of Vorarlberg, before the border with West Germany, there are more mountains. But the province also has beautiful wooded valleys and rare varieties of alpine flowers.

TYROL

Tyrol is a province which is famous for winter sports. The provincial capital is the city of Innsbruck.

Tyrol earns more foreign currency from tourism than any other Austrian province. Each year Tyrol caters for eight times as many people as actually live there. The province is

A typical Tyrolean scene

called the "land of mountains" because of the magnificent scenery dominated by the Alps and the Kitzbühel Slate Mountains. Communications have been made easier with the construction of the Inn Valley Motorway and the Brenner Motorway; the latter makes travel south to Italy much quicker. In 1978 the 14-kilometre (9-mile) Arlberg Road Tunnel was completed and this provided the first all-weather road link between Vorarlberg and Tyrol.

Tyrol is an important producer of hydro-electric power. In the past, the province's prosperity was based on several products: timber, which was floated down the River Inn to the Danube; wool; leather; horn; and silver from the mines

17

A section of the Brenner Motorway. Since its construction, driving south to Italy has become much easier and quicker

at Schwaz. Tyrol has wonderful churches, and public buildings, and splendid old taverns dating from this affluent period and, of course, they help to attract tourists today. The province is popular with tourists throughout the year. Winter sports enthusiasts arrive for the snow. In the spring, summer and autumn ramblers enjoy walking on the hillsides and in the valleys covered with flowers. The lakes of Walchsee, Achensee and Schwarzsee (*See* means "lake" in German) are popular with swimmers; and sunbathing is common when the temperature is high and the sun is strong.

SALZBURG LAND

The province of Salzburg Land is the lakeland of Austria. Salt has been mined there for many centuries and salt gave the city and the province its name. The city of Salzburg is the provincial capital. (*Salz* means "salt" in German).

Picturesque villages such as this one can be seen throughout Austria

The province comprises limestone alps, the lakes of the western Salzkammergut and the eastern part of the Kitzbühel Alps. Small towns, such as Zell am See and Kaprun, are winter sports centres. Kaprun has a fixed-rail cable-car and an ordinary cable-car to carry visitors up to the Kitzsteinhorn glacier. The skiing facilities there can be used all the year round.

The vast range of the Tauern Mountains, which reach nearly 4,000 metres (13,000 feet), used to cut the province off from the south of the country but a road and tunnel built in the Grossglockner Pass in the twentieth century have improved communications.

The Glockner-Kaprun project is part of the Tauern hydro-

A view of Salzburg

Lake Wolfgang in the Salzkammergut

electric complex—one of the largest hydro-electric plants in Europe. The province of Salzburg Land is an important agricultural region of Austria, especially on the plain to the north of the provincial capital.

CARINTHIA

Carinthia is Austria's most southerly province. The west of Carinthia is mountainous and contains Austria's highest mountain—the Grossglockner. The east is lower-lying. The

21

area around the provincial capital of Klagenfurt includes lakes such as the Wörther See, the Ossiacher See and the Millstätter See, and is popular with visitors. There are two hundred smaller lakes in the province and excellent facilities for aquatic sports such as water skiing and wind-surfing. Carinthia is heavily forested and timber is the province's most important natural resource. Iron ore, lead, tungsten, zinc and magnesite (used to make magnesium) are mined in the mountains.

The town of Villach, close to the borders with Italy and Yugoslavia, is the most important rail and road junction in the eastern Alps.

In the lowland valleys the climate is mild and sunny. Fruits such as peaches, grapes and apricots are grown and sunflowers are cultivated to produce cooking oil.

STYRIA

The province of Styria, in the centre and south-east of the country, is Austria's green province. Extensive forests cover at least half the area. The timber produced is used for housing, furniture and paper-making. A further quarter of the land area is given over to vineyards where grapes are grown, and to alpine pastures providing grazing for cattle, horses and sheep.

Styria is Austria's main mining province. Iron ore is mined in the mountains in the north—ninety per cent of all the country's iron ore comes from the Erzberg (meaning "ore

A magnesite plant in Carinthia

mountain"). Lignite (brown coal) is mined in the west and there are also deposits of magnesite which is exported to many countries.

The economy of the province is based on several important industries, including iron and steel-making, engineering, cellulose and paper-making and the manufacture of electrical goods. Motor vehicles are made in the provincial capital of Graz.

The climate of Styria is pleasant with long summers. The snowy peaks of the Styrian Alps are popular with hunters and fishermen.

23

UPPER AUSTRIA

Upper Austria is a hilly province. The River Danube flows through the province and in the south-west there is a lake-studded area called the Salzkammergut. Agriculture is important in the hill region. The province also produces oil and natural gas. At Steyr is the Daimler-Puch plant which produces tractors, trucks and ball-bearings. Austria's largest aluminium plant is located in the province and, in addition, Lenzing is a major centre for the manufacture of cellulose and wood-fibre.

Villages in the north of Upper Austria are very small and many farms are tiny. The south of the province is more prosperous; here the villages and towns are larger. Wels, for instance, is an old town with an historic town centre and industrial suburbs. The provincial capital, Linz, is in the north, on the Danube.

LOWER AUSTRIA

The largest Austrian province is Lower Austria which, despite its name, is situated in the north-east of the country. The provincial capital, Vienna, is also a province in its own right and, further, the national capital.

Much of the country's wheat, sugar beet and grapes for winemaking are grown in Lower Austria. Increasingly, however, the region's natural resources are being exploited and new industries developed. Austria's largest oil-fields lie to the north of the River Danube and there are also many industrial

24

centres where textiles, foodstuffs, chemicals, iron and other metals are processed. Hydro-electric schemes have been developed on the Danube to help meet the increased demand for power.

The River Danube flows through Upper Austria on its way to the Black Sea in Romania. To the north of the river there are orchards and vineyards. In the mountains near the border with Czechoslovakia there are medieval forts and castles. In the south, winter sports resorts, such as Mariazell and Semmering, are frequented by Austrians rather than visitors from abroad.

Mariazell, a popular winter sports resort in Lower Austria

A view of the town of Durnstein on the River Danube, where Richard the Lionheart was once imprisoned

Wiener Neustadt is a very old city in Lower Austria (although its German name means "new town"). It has adapted itself to the needs of the latter half of the twentieth century and produces locomotives, leather and machinery.

Lower Austria has a long and impressive history. The River Danube provides access to Hungary and the Black Sea in the east, so trading centres grew up along its banks to cater for the merchants and their ships. The rulers of Austria built their homes in the area and there are still many medieval castles and palaces built by emperors and princes. The

26

English king, Richard the Lionheart, was imprisoned in the town of Dürnstein. His whereabouts were discovered by the minstrel Blondel, but the King was released only after a high ransom had been paid.

BURGENLAND

The province of Burgenland in the east of the country is an agricultural region producing wheat, maize, vegetables, fruit and wine. There are canning factories near the main centres of agricultural production.

The small provincial capital is Eisenstadt. Burgenland—the "land of castles"—was part of Hungary until the end of the First World War. Many people from Vienna build holiday-homes in the province.

Austrian History

Austria is in the geographical centre of Europe—a fact which has influenced much of its history. The country has been inhabited for thousands of years. In the Iron Age—between 1000 and 400 BC—it was inhabited by the Illyrians who achieved a high standard of civilization. They were followed by the Celts, then by the Romans who, at the time of Christ, made the Danube and the alpine regions part of their empire. The Roman province of Noricum included much of present-day Austria. The Romans built roads and established camps and settlements which later developed into Austrian cities. The Roman town of Vindobona eventually became Vienna, Juvavum became Salzburg and Lentia became Linz.

Christianity began to spread throughout the province from about AD 300. About a century later, Noricum was raided by Germanic tribes and the Romans withdrew to Italy. The Germanic invaders brought their own language and customs. The region was subjected to repeated invasions and upheavals between AD 500 and 700, as the power of the Germanic tribesmen was replaced, in turn, by that of the Huns and the Avars—warlike nomads from Asia.

At the end of the eighth century, Charlemagne, the King of the Franks, drove out the Avars and established a border

The remains of the amphitheatre in the Roman settlement of Carnuntum in Lower Austria

province to defend his empire in the east, including central Germany which he had conquered. In 880 the province was overrun by the Magyars, a formidable tribe from Hungary. But in 955, the empire-builder Otto the Great defeated the Hungarians and re-occupied the territory.

Leopold von Babenburg was made the ruler of Austria in 976 and his family continued to rule for two hundred and seventy years. There was a period of peaceful development under the Babenburgs. Silver, gold and salt were mined. Religious orders founded monasteries in the east of the

29

Burg Forchtenstein, built around 1300, when the rule of the Habsburg family in Austria was just beginning

country and these became centres of learning and culture. Austria lay on the crusaders' route to the Holy Land, so people became used to seeing travellers from other countries. Important nobles built castles at strategic points. In the year 996 the word *Ostarrichi* was used for the first time in a document, and this developed into the present German name for Austria—*Österreich*. The last of the Babenburgs, Frederick the Quarrelsome, was killed in battle against the Magyars in the middle of the thirteenth century.

Duke Rudolf was the first member of the Habsburg family to rule Austria. He became Holy Roman Emperor and Duke of Austria in 1273. Several countries belonged to the Holy Roman Empire and the ruler of one of the member countries was always elected emperor—or principal ruler. The Habsburgs ruled as the royal family in Austria for six hundred and forty years. There were twenty emperors and kings during their time and their power and influence were enormous.

In 1440 Frederick III became Holy Roman Emperor and from that time, until the end of the Holy Roman Empire in 1806, every emperor (apart from two) was a Habsburg. Spain, the Netherlands, Hungary and part of Italy were added to the Habsburg lands by marriage alliances.

The Hofburg in Innsbruck, once an imperial palace of the Habsburgs

Then, in the sixteenth and seventeenth centuries the Turks began to push their way westwards and huge Turkish armies laid siege unsuccessfully to Vienna. With the defeat of the Turks, Austria became a major power in central Europe. Nevertheless, the Habsburgs (who were Roman Catholics) were often in conflict with Protestants living in the German states and in the early seventeenth century this resulted in the Thirty Years War.

Some time later, in 1740, Empress Maria Theresa became ruler of the lands of the Habsburg family. She reigned for forty years and had sixteen children. She attempted to unite the various kingdoms into one joint empire with the aid of a strong army of soldiers recruited from all over the empire. She improved industry and trade, abolished torture and made provision for schooling. Her son, Joseph II, continued her policy of trying to unite all the separate kingdoms. He tried to rule the whole empire from Vienna and wanted to impose the same laws on all the states. This led to a rebellion in Hungary. Nevertheless, he abolished serfdom and introduced freedom of religion for everyone.

Joseph's nephew, Francis II, was the last Holy Roman Emperor. In 1804, he changed his title to Emperor of Austria for, by that time, the Holy Roman Empire no longer had any power. Francis lost lands during wars with the French led by Napoleon but retrieved them later. Austria was at war with France during the Napoleonic Wars (1793–1815) and after 1805 Austria was actually occupied by the French. In 1809, however, an Austrian army defeated Napoleon at the Battle of Aspern. But the tide soon turned and a French victory followed. After Napoleon's defeat by the British and their allies at Waterloo, in 1815, much of the prestige of Austria was restored under the Treaty of Vienna. Austria regained territory in the north of Italy and led the newly-formed German Confederation. She became one of the leading powers in Europe in the nineteenth century.

During the first part of the century there was much industrial progress in Austria. The Austrian National Bank was founded in 1816. The first railway in Austria was opened in 1837.

From 1809, Prince Metternich was the Chancellor of Austria. Metternich disapproved of nationalism and freedom for the peoples of the empire. The Austrian Empire still ruled several different nations and he did not want to lose control of them. Nationalist ideas in Hungary, Bohemia (Czechoslovakia) and Croatia (Yugoslavia) were kept under control, but the Italians in Lombardy tried to end Austrian rule. By 1848 there were attempts at revolution all over the Austrian Empire but the Austrian army overcame the revolutionaries.

The Emperor Francis Joseph ruled the Austrian Empire from 1848 until 1916—for sixty-eight years. He became emperor when he was only eighteen, during the mid-nineteenth century revolutions. He was forced to give up lands in Germany and Italy when his armies were defeated. In 1867 he reached agreement with the Hungarians who were allowed to have their own government and parliament; they accepted one army for the entire empire and agreed that the name of the state was to be Austria-Hungary.

In June 1914, Archduke Francis Ferdinand, who was the heir to the Habsburg throne of Austria, was killed at Sarajevo by a Serbian nationalist (Serbia was later to become part of Yugoslavia) who was dissatisfied with rule by Austrians. The government of Austria thought that Serbia itself was to blame for the murder, and this event sparked off the First World War. The Austrians were defeated and, after the war, the empire broke up and the dependent countries of the Austrian Empire then became independent of Austrian dominance; huge parts of the former empire are now part of Czechoslovakia, Hungary, Italy, Yugoslavia, Romania and Poland.

The Austrian Empire had been very large and powerful but people in different parts of the empire had little in common with each other—they were more concerned with the interests of their particular nation than with the affairs of the empire. Finally, in 1918, the Austrians themselves decided that they no longer wanted an emperor, and the country became a republic. The new Republic of Austria retained only one quarter of the old Austrian Empire and had no outlet to the sea. The country had difficulty maintaining its independence and had serious economic problems. At first the boundaries with Hungary, Czechoslovakia and Yugoslavia remained closed. Food was in short supply, prices were high and the poor, especially, suffered from disease during the harsh winter of 1920–21. The country was helped by loans from the League of Nations, inflation was checked and the currency was changed by introducing the schilling as the monetary unit of Austria.

Then there were political disagreements in the country and paramilitary organisations began to emerge. The country remained troubled and uneasy. In 1933, the Lower House

The Parliament building in Vienna, with the *Rathaus* (City Hall) behind it

of the Austrian Parliament ceased to govern and power was taken over by the Chancellor, Engelbert Dollfuss. This was the end, for the time being, of democracy in Austria. The Austrian Nazi (National Socialist) Party was growing and, in 1934, its members tried unsuccessfully to seize power. These National Socialists were given support by Hitler's regime in Germany. But, during this uprising, Dollfuss was murdered and was followed by Kurt Schuschnigg who met with Adolf Hitler in February 1938. In the following month German troops crossed the border into Austria and occupied the country as part of Hitler's aim to unite German-speaking countries. Austria lost its independence and became part of the German Reich. In effect, Austria ceased to exist. Within eighteen months of this event the Second World War had begun. Austria therefore entered the war on the side of Germany and was badly bombed by the Allies. Austria was occupied by Germany until 1945 when it was liberated by the Allies. There were resistance movements in Austria throughout the war years and these were especially active towards the end of the war.

The liberation of Austria began at the end of March 1945 when Russian troops entered the country from the east, and American and British forces arrived in the west. The country was in a state of chaos and much of Vienna was destroyed. A provisional government was formed under Karl Renner in April and even then there was still fighting in parts of the country. The second Republic of Austria was formed and the democratic constitution has been in force since 1 May 1945.

After the war, Austria was occupied by Allied forces—it was ten years before she regained her full independence in 1955. The four occupying powers—Britain, France, Russia and the United States of America—each looked after a zone of Austria.

In the State Treaty of 1955 the four occupying powers recognized Austria as an independent and democratic state. The treaty forbade political or economic union with Germany, protected the rights of minority groups of Slovenes and Croats living in Austria, banned fascist and National Socialist groups and ensured that only those members of the house of Habsburg who were willing to renounce all their rights to confiscated property were allowed to remain in Austria.

Austrians understood that they needed to be self-sufficient politically and this awoke in them a national consciousness and a deep need to maintain independence. Austria is now an independent, neutral country. In order to maintain permanent neutrality Austria has decided not to join any military alliance or to allow military bases to be established by foreign troops on her soil, and not to side with any of the major powers in the event of troubles or war. Austria tries to establish and maintain good relations with all other countries, pursues peaceful policies and is active within the United Nations. The construction of the Vienna International Centre has made the capital of Austria into an important meeting-place for United Nations discussions.

Transport in a Land of Mountains

Austria's transportation systems suffer from many problems similar to those of the neighbouring mountainous country of Switzerland. Each country has high mountain ranges which tend to cut off the people of one valley from those of nearby valleys. Nevertheless, there is a well-developed transport network that reaches into remote alpine areas.

It is not just a question of building roads and railways. The Neutor road tunnel, for instance, is cut through solid rock and connects the centre of Salzburg with one of its suburbs. The tunnel, which is 123 metres (400 feet) long, was constructed as long ago as 1767. Elsewhere in Austria the entrance to a road tunnel may suddenly appear on a mountain road.

The process of improving the transportation system in this country of mountains is a long and expensive one. The edges of most roads in the Alps are fitted with guard-rails to help keep cars on the road. Where there is snow on the roads, studded tyres are allowed between November and April. On very steep, snow-covered gradients snow-chains are needed on tyres.

Sometimes there are heavy falls of snow during winter which bring temporary chaos to the roads and railways. Avalanches of snow, rocks and earth may thunder down the

38

This rather odd-looking construction is the ventilation shaft and entrance to a road tunnel through the mountains

slopes of a mountain, so that buildings and trees are swept away. Some avalanches are landslides. A sound—even a shout—can be enough to start an avalanche. Powder avalanches are caused when strong winter winds whirl dry snow down the steep mountain slopes. Sometimes trees are planted to minimize the danger to buildings and life. Where a potential avalanche has become particularly dangerous, it may be started deliberately by firing a gun to make it slip before it becomes even larger.

Austria's geographical location in Europe gives the country's nationalized railway system a central importance. In addition, the Arlberg Tunnel in the west and the Tauern Tunnel through the Alps on the Salzburg to Villach line ease communication problems within the country.

There are good roads throughout Austria and the *Autobahn*

39

(or motorway) from Munich (in Germany) to Vienna has 320 kilometres (200 miles) of its total length in Austria. It passes close to Salzburg, and to the lakes of the Salzkammergut and Linz. Another motorway is being built to link Vienna with Villach in Carinthia and then with the Italian frontier.

Since the River Danube which flows through the northern part of the country is a broad river there are few bridges spanning its width; but it can be crossed by means of car ferries at many different points. These are merely a continuation of the road system.

For journeys abroad and the export of goods Austrian Airlines fly passengers and freight to most countries in Europe and the Middle East. In addition, more than thirty foreign national airlines operate regular flights from many parts of the world to Austrian airports; and there are services run by many more charter companies. Vienna Airport is the most important in the country but Austria has six commercial airports, and there are internal air services which operate between Vienna, Innsbruck, Salzburg, Klagenfurt, Graz and Linz.

Vienna

Vienna is the capital city of Austria. It is two thousand years old. The Romans built the fortress of Vindobona on a small Celtic settlement sited where Vienna now stands, surrounded by wooded mountains. The city is situated in the east of Austria, on the River Danube, between the two mountain ranges of the Alps in the west and the Carpathians in the east.

Vienna has a population in excess of 1,600,000; almost one Austrian in every four is Viennese. The city is justly proud of its beautiful buildings, many of which are very old. The most important church in Vienna is St Stephen's Cathedral. It has a tall and slender Gothic spire. The cathedral was damaged during the Second World War and its steep roof, with a pattern of coloured tiles on the exterior surface, had to be rebuilt. The north tower houses the largest bell in Austria; it weighs 21 tonnes.

The Viennese Palace of Schönbrunn (the name means "beautiful fountain") is often called the most beautiful palace in Europe. It was once the summer home of the Habsburg family. State banquets and official receptions are held in its splendid rooms. The palace also houses an impressive coach museum containing coaches used by former members of the Habsburg family—including small coaches (for the young children of the family) which were drawn by two sheep. Schönbrunn today includes a zoo, and a palmhouse which is the largest hothouse in Europe. The palace itself contains more than 1,400 rooms, but only about forty of these are now on view to the public.

Vienna is known as a city of music. The Opera House is famous throughout the world. The Concert Hall is where the Vienna Symphony Orchestra plays programmes of classical music but also where famous pop groups have given concerts.

A mosaic of the Habsburg coat-of-arms on the roof of St. Stephen's Cathedral in Vienna

The baroque splendour of the Palace of Schönbrunn

The Vienna Festival of Music and Drama is held in the city each summer; it includes concerts, operas and plays. This was the city of Haydn, Mozart, Beethoven, Schubert and the two Strausses. The city has choral societies, orchestras, an opera and a famous boys' choir—the Vienna Boys' Choir— which sings at Mass each Sunday morning in the Hofburg Chapel. There are actually four separate boys' choirs, one of which, in turn, is always on a world tour.

In central Vienna there is little modern architecture

43

Members of the world-famous Vienna Boys' Choir

because many historic buildings have been carefully preserved.
The University of Vienna is more than six hundred years old.
It is the oldest university in any German-speaking country.
The most notable modern buildings in the centre are the
Francis Joseph railway station (comprising a railway station,
a computer centre and a university in one building) and the
new United Nations building. But in its outer parts Vienna is a
modern city where many housing estates have been built, and
it has a modern underground railway system.

The old fortified town walls of Vienna were pulled down in

44

the nineteenth century and replaced by the famous tree-lined road called the Ringstrasse. This curves around central Vienna in the shape of a horse-shoe. There are several parks on this road and one of them, the Stadtpark, contains a marble statue of Johann Strauss playing a violin. The little house in which, in 1867, he composed the waltz, *The Blue Danube*, can still be seen. In fact, the Danube now flows only through the suburbs of the city. The water in the city centre is really a canal.

The famous Prater of Vienna is a forest park in the city centre. It is more than two hundred years old, and has funfairs, cafes and sporting facilities. These include a golf course, a trotting race-course, a bicycle-racing track, a stadium which holds 72,000 spectators and a swimming-pool. The funfair has a huge ferris wheel which takes ten minutes to make one complete revolution.

Vienna has many other large and well-designed parks. The Vienna Woods—an area of forested hills to the west of the city—are close at hand and many people enjoy walking in them to see the wild flowers in the spring and the colours of the trees in autumn. The Vienna Woods are mainly beech forest, with plantations of silver birch as well as oak, poplar, elm, maple and aspen. This is a favourite outing from the capital for a picnic in the fresh air. There are also several taverns in the woods where local wines are served.

The Hofburg was once the imperial town palace of the Habsburgs. It is a group of buildings in central Vienna which includes the Treasure Chamber where the Crown Jewels are stored, as well as the regalia of the Holy Roman Empire, including the thousand-year-old crown of the Emperors. The Hofburg also includes the Imperial State Apartments and the Spanish Riding School with its large white riding hall. Here the public can now watch the horses and riders performing. The horses are very carefully trained and they move gracefully in time to music.

The city of Vienna can boast magnificent architecture as well as art galleries and museums containing many treasures. It is a city of colourful palaces and baroque churches which are highly decorated with elaborate painted ceilings and gilded statues of angels, saints and cherubs set amongst

The monument to the composer Johann Strauss, in the Stadtpark, Vienna

Horses and riders demonstrate their skill at the Spanish Riding School in Vienna

marble pillars. The Museum of Fine Arts is one of the most famous picture galleries in Europe. It contains the largest collection of Breughel paintings in the world, as well as paintings by Rubens, Rembrandt, Velasquez and Dürer. In addition, the Austrian Gallery in the Belvedere Palace displays paintings by nineteenth- and twentieth-century artists.

The capital is also an important shopping centre. The Mariahilferstrasse is Vienna's longest shopping street with more than five kilometres (three miles) of shops.

47

Other Cities and Towns

BREGENZ

Bregenz, capital of the province of Vorarlberg, has a population of about 25,000. Behind the town is the Pfaender Mountain. Its summit is at 1,066 metres (3,500 feet) and this can be reached by cable-car in seven minutes. The town is sometimes referred to as the "port of entry" into Austria, since it is situated on the shore of Lake Constance; and steamers travel backwards and forwards across the lake between Austria, Switzerland and Germany.

The museum in Bregenz proudly features mosaics dating from its Roman days. The town is also known for its annual summer music festival. For this, a huge stage has been constructed on piles in the lake. The plays and operas performed on this stage are watched by audiences from the shores of the lake. When Mozart's opera *Il Seraglio* was performed, one of the singers came onto the stage from a boat.

INNSBRUCK

Innsbruck, capital of the province of Tyrol, has 100,000 inhabitants. It is a beautiful city with an ancient university and superb views of towering mountains. There are attractive buildings in the old town, where cafes provide concerts and

A view of Innsbruck, from the clock tower

traditional beer-cellars resound with singing and dancing.

The city has an Alpine Zoo which contains rare animals and birds usually seen in the wild only by mountaineers. It is easy to reach the mountains near Innsbruck since a funicular (a railway worked by a cable and a stationary engine) takes only five minutes to reach Hungerburg at an altitude of 915 metres (3,000 feet) and from there a cable-car journey of a quarter of an hour takes visitors to Hafelekar at an altitude of 2,260 metres (7,400 feet).

Maria Theresa Street is the famous main street of Innsbruck, behind which rise the jagged limestone peaks of the Nordkette range.

The Innsbruck Folk Museum shows the life of the Austrian farmer throughout the centuries.

A tramcar in Maria Theresa Street in Innsbruck. The mountains in the background are part of the Nordkette range

SALZBURG

The city of Salzburg, capital of the province of Salzburg Land, has 145,000 inhabitants. The city is spacious with palaces, mansions, squares, fountains and fascinating winding streets in the centre. Apart from its museums, exhibitions and music festival, Salzburg is also a city where people go to take a "cure", because of the local deposits of curative mud, the mineral waters and brine. The mud treatment improves rheumatic conditions; brine baths guard against respiratory ailments, and mineral waters are beneficial for stomach disorders.

Salzburg was once the home of Mozart. His opera *The*

Magic Flute was first performed there. It is an old city which has been preserved with great care and is very popular with tourists. The famous Salzburg Festival is held annually in the summer.

KLAGENFURT

Klagenfurt, capital of the province of Carinthia, has a population of 86,000. It has an unusual open-air museum containing a miniature collection of some of the most famous buildings throughout the world. The main square of Klagenfurt is lined with chestnut trees and in the centre stands a dragon, spouting water. The dragon was carved out of rock at the end of the sixteenth century. A century later, a statue of

A view of Salzburg, with its castle and some of its many old buildings

Hercules carrying a spiked club was added. There is also a dragon on the town's coat-of-arms.

Klagenfurt looks rather different from the other provincial capitals because its architecture has been influenced by its nearness to Italy. It is an important centre for the marketing of the mineral and farm products of Carinthia.

LINZ

Linz, capital of the province of Upper Austria, has a population of 200,000. It is the third largest city in Austria—after Vienna and Graz. The River Danube runs through the centre of Linz. Parts of the old city have attractive courtyards and merchants' houses from previous centuries. Linz boasts two

The house in Salzburg where Mozart was born in 1756

The *Landhaus*, or seat of local government, in Klagenfurt

cathedrals, and the oldest church in Austria—St. Martin's, which dates from the eighth century. It also has a castle—now a museum.

It was in Linz that Mozart composed a symphony in a great hurry, to be performed at a local concert. This symphony (Number 36) is still known as the "Linz Symphony".

Linz is an important centre for the production of iron, steel and chemicals. The largest industrial concern in Austria, the United Austrian Iron and Steel Works, employing 80,000, has its main plant at Linz. The firm produces iron, steel, sheet-metal and wire (as well as complete steel production plants), and these are exported all over the world.

Graz

Graz, capital of the province of Styria, is Austria's second largest city and has a population of 240,000. It is a city of courtyards, narrow streets, old houses and attractive squares. The main square of the city has a market each day.

Graz is the home of an armoury housed in a four-storey building dating from 1640. The contents—more than 30,000 items—were catalogued in the nineteenth century. There are helmets, guns, pistols, powder horns, cannons and complete suits of armour, as well as armour for tournaments and jousting.

This Clock-Tower is the symbol of the Styrian capital of Graz

One unusual feature of Graz is that old dungeons in the town have been converted into a summer theatre—the former cells now being used to seat the audience. Operas, plays and concerts can all be enjoyed in Graz. (This is the town to which Franz Schubert dedicated his "Unfinished" symphony.) In addition, in the summer, the grounds of Castle Eggenberg are a popular place for visitors. Peacocks and silver pheasants roam at will in the gardens, and deer graze in the now drained moat.

EISENSTADT

Eisenstadt, capital of the province of Burgenland, has a population of 10,000. It is situated 40 kilometres (25 miles) from Vienna. It has a castle of yellow sandstone, which was once the town house of the Esterhazy family—one of the most influential families in Austro-Hungary which did much to encourage the talents of aspiring musicians. Eisenstadt was the home of the eighteenth-century composer Joseph Haydn. For thirty years he conducted Prince Esterhazy's orchestra and, when he died, he was buried in the hillside church of Eisenstadt.

The capitals of the Austrian provinces are all very much smaller than the national capital—Vienna—with its population of 1,600,000. Bregenz is only one quarter the size of Innsbruck and one eighth the size of Linz. Eisenstadt, with a population of 10,000, is clearly very different from Salzburg with 145,000. Yet these provincial capitals are all important centres compared with many of the smaller towns of the country.

In the westerly provinces of Vorarlberg and Tyrol there are many resorts that are popular with foreign tourists as well as with Austrians. Some are towns and others large villages but all are bustling centres for holidaymakers and visitors during the winter, the summer or throughout the year. In Tyrol these resorts include Seefeld, Igls, Kitzbühel, Mayrhofen and St. Anton. In Salzburg Land, too, there are many popular centres including Bad Gastein and Zell am See.

In the province of Carinthia there are beautiful mountain lakes within the Tauern Range and glaciers in the north of

This castle in Eisenstadt once belonged to the influential Esterhazy family

A general view of the resort of Seefeld in Tyrol

the province, as well as attractive holiday towns such as
Millstatt built on the shore of the Millstättersee. Numerous
resorts have been developed near or on the shores of mountain
lakes in the Salzkammergut region, most of which is situated
in Upper Austria. Amongst the most famous of these resorts
are Bad Ischl, St. Wolfgang and Gmunden.

Village Life

About twenty per cent of the area of Austria is arable land where crops are grown. A further twenty-nine per cent of the country is used for pasture. There are thousands of farms, the majority of them very small. Although fewer people now work on farms than was the case twenty years ago, the value of farm produce has more than doubled during this period due to mechanization. The farms of Austria supply about ninety per cent of the country's food. Production of animal fats, beef and cheese exceeds home demand, and surplus food is exported.

The main farming areas are the regions to the north of the Alps and on both banks of the River Danube, extending to the plains of the eastern borders. Crops are grown, cattle are reared, and orchards and vines are cultivated. On the lower slopes of the mountains the main occupation is cattle farming. In the forest areas timber is an important product and export. The main forests of Austria are in the south.

The principal crops are wheat, barley, maize, potatoes and sugar beet. The most important livestock are cattle, pigs, horses and poultry. Whether a farm is small, medium-sized or large it is likely to be run as a family concern. Specialized forestry, however, is mainly run by large-scale state-owned

58

Haymaking in Tyrol

companies, or companies run by the federal provinces, local committees, the church or co-operatives. The main forests are spruce and pine. Sawmills and factories process the timber and many Austrians are employed in them.

Austria's foodstuffs industry is an important part of the

A typical Austrian country scene. Cattle-farming is one of the most important parts of Austrian agriculture

economy. Dairy production (including dried milk, preserved milk products and cheese) is common in the area of Lake Constance in the west, the Inn valley in Tyrol, the northern alpine foothills and Styria. Much of the sugar beet is grown (and sugar beet factories sited) in the east of Lower Austria and Burgenland. There is a confectionery industry in the large centres, particularly in Vienna. The flat farmlands in the east of Austria, between Vienna and Lake Neusiedl, are the centre of the canning industry. The values of Austrian food-stuff production in descending order of importance are meat, brewing, confectionery, dairy produce and sugar.

There are vineyards in all parts of the country, and the

60

wine produced in Burgenland is especially fruity because of the mild, sunny climate in the east. The quality of a wine depends on the climate of the region, the soil, and the type of grape, as well as on the skill of the grape-grower. Climatic factors which affect grape-growing are temperature, moisture and duration of sunshine. Even small variations in seasonal weather from one region to another affect the quality of the harvested grapes.

The history of the Austrian vineyards is a long one, extending as far back as the pre-Christian era when the Celts planted vines along the Danube. The growing of grapes became more

Part of the Wine Museum in Krems (Lower Austria), showing an old wine-press and various storage jars

important when the Romans occupied the area. Archaeologists have found Roman wine-presses and clay drinking vessels for wine. In the Middle Ages the monks in the monasteries carried on the tradition of growing grapes to make wine. Most of the wine comes from Lower Austria (in the north-east) and much of it is white wine, although some red wines are produced south of Vienna.

Of the wine produced in Austria (about 30 million cases annually) most is consumed within the country but about two million cases are exported. Germany is the largest importer of Austrian wines. Austrian wine is also sold in Britain, Switzerland, Sweden, Denmark, the Netherlands, Belgium, Canada and the United States of America.

The scenery of the Austrian countryside is extremely varied—ranging from impressive alpine areas to wooded highlands; from flat plains to fertile valleys; from wooded slopes to extensive meadows. Some of the villages take their names from a nearby town. Not far from the town of Bad Gastein, in Salzburg Land, for instance, is the alpine village of Dorfgastein, at the lower end of the valley. Close to the town of Millstatt in Carinthia province is the village of Obermillstatt, set high up on the hillside amongst meadows.

There are numerous farming villages set amongst fields, orchards and wooded hills. Some fields are full of sunflowers which are grown for the oil of their seeds. Elsewhere, single poles are stuck in the ground and hay is wound round them for drying. Other poles are placed horizontally to make a

Hay wound round poles for drying

simple fence on which the hay is hung to be dried. Both systems lift the hay off the ground and allow the fresh air to it; otherwise it might rot in rainy weather. Many hay fields have a small wooden hut in which hay is stored. The farmers use this hay to feed the cattle during winter when there is snow on the ground.

About half a million Austrians work on small farms throughout the country. The farmhouse may be a very simple affair with a living-room and kitchen on the ground floor, and a

63

ladder leading through a hole in the ceiling to the bedrooms
upstairs.

The approach road to a village often features a wayside
shrine with a thatched or wooden roof. The villagers place
flowers on these shrines. About half the population of Austria
lives in small villages.

Government

The head of state in Austria is the Federal President who is elected directly by the people for a six-year term of office. Voting is compulsory in Austrian presidential elections. The Federal President appoints the Prime Minister and also members of the cabinet. He represents the Republic internationally and has the power to dissolve the Lower House of Parliament.

There are two houses of parliament—the Lower House (the Nationalrat) and the Upper House (the Bundesrat). The members of the Lower House are elected for a four-year term in a secret ballot by a system of proportional representation. Anyone aged nineteen or more has a vote. The members of the Upper House are elected by the provincial parliaments, the proportion of members depending on the size of population in each province. The powers of this Upper House are rather greater than those of the British House of Lords, and more like those of the United States Senate. Bills approved by the Lower House must be presented to the Upper House which can object to the proposed legislation. But if the Lower House again carries its original resolution it is then passed and becomes part of the law of the land.

The government is led by the Prime Minister (who has the

title of Federal Chancellor in Austria). He is usually the leader of the strongest party. Austria is a parliamentary democracy under the federal constitution of 1920.

Since Austria is a federal state each of the nine provinces in the country has its own constitution. The parliaments of these provinces send representatives to the Upper House of Parliament.

For many years there was a coalition between the two main political parties by which they agreed to run the country jointly. But, by 1966, the People's Party had a majority of the seats in the Lower House. The main parties, in order of popularity, are now the Socialist Party (Social Democrats) and the People's Party (Christian Democrats), followed— a long way behind—by the Freedom Party (Liberals). The Socialist Party was founded in 1889. It has held a parliamentary majority, and so formed the government in Austria, since 1970. The party seeks to end class distinctions, to achieve a fair distribution of the rewards of labour and a situation in which people work together for a better society. It draws its main supporters from the wage- and salary-earners in Austria and works closely with the Austrian Trade Union Federation.

The People's Party was founded in 1945. It is a Christian-Democrat party founded on the principle of social integration and emphasises the common interest of the various sections of society. The party wishes to establish a society in which people see themselves as partners.

The *Rathaus* (City Hall) in Vienna. Every year the Vienna Festival is officially opened here

The Freedom Party was founded in 1955. It has appeal to those who value personal achievement and the responsibilities of freedom, rather than collective security.

Education in Austria

There is a long tradition of education in Austria. Compulsory education for children up to the age of fourteen was introduced as early as 1867. Changes in the educational system in Austria in the 1960s led to an increase in the types of schools available, dependent on ability and interests. The government tries to make sure that students of equal ability have equal opportunities to receive higher education, irrespective of family background; and also that everyone has the chance to choose (or transfer) to the kind of schooling best suited to his particular preference and abilities.

Austrian schooling begins at six years of age and basic compulsory education now lasts for nine years: four years at primary school (*Volksschule*) and four years at secondary school (*Hauptschule*) where pupils receive a broad general education. The ninth and final year of basic education is a polytechnic-type course which prepares students for the practicalities of life.

If a child plans to go on to university after schooling is completed then he or she may, instead, go straight to a *Gymnasium* or *Realgymnasium* for eight years after the four primary years. The *Gymnasium* has a bias towards arts subjects; the *Realgymnasium* is orientated to natural science.

68

The main school holidays are at Christmas, Easter and in the summer, during July and August. Most children spend a week on several occasions during their school career learning to ski under instruction in the mountains.

School education in Austria is provided free for all pupils. Since 1971 transport costs to and from school have also been paid by the state and, since 1972, school books have been provided free of charge. Financial support in the form of grants is provided for the children of needy parents so that

A beginners' ski class for school-children

they can continue their education after the years of compulsory schooling. The School Education Act of 1974 encouraged more effective co-operation between teachers, parents and pupils who now have equal representation on the school community committees, and this has resulted in an increased interest in education.

After leaving full-time school some pupils embark on apprenticeships where they learn a skilled trade while continuing part-time schooling as well. The vocational school system allows a student to leave school and begin work at a variety of ages. Some begin a form of vocational training for a particular job from the age of fourteen or fifteen. They then finish their school careers with a year's course to prepare them for the transition to a working life.

Since 1972 attendance at an Austrian university has been free both for Austrians and for students from developing countries. There are now over 100,000 university and college students in Austria. Of these, as many as 12,000 come from abroad. These large numbers of foreign students are attracted by the range of courses offered and the high standards achieved in Austrian universities. In addition to the dozen or so universities, there are six colleges of art and music which have university status.

The University of Vienna was founded in 1365 and is now the oldest university in the German-speaking world. Other Austrian universities also have long traditions, as is the case with the University of Graz, the University of Innsbruck and

The Academy of Science in the University of Vienna

the University of Salzburg. The Technical University of Vienna specializes in courses in science and technology. The University of Agriculture and Forestry is also in Vienna, as are the Veterinary University and the Economics University. The University of Linz specializes in sociology, economics and business management. The University of Education is at Klagenfurt.

The Austrian Academy of Sciences is the most prestigious body in Austrian intellectual life. Its members, both from Austria and abroad, work in the arts, mathematics and the sciences. There are also close on three hundred learned societies in Austria which organize lectures and conferences and produce magazines and journals to spread information as widely as possible. The country has many public libraries

71

as well as scientific collections of books and periodicals. There are libraries of old books at the monasteries of Melk and Admont. The Austrian National Library in Vienna dates from 1526 and contains more than two million printed works and twenty-eight thousand hand-written manuscripts, as well as collections of maps, music manuscripts, papyrus scrolls and photographs.

The Austrian Court and State Archives in Vienna contain one of the world's most important collections of historical state documents (after the collections in the Vatican and the Archives Nationales in Paris). Some of these documents date back to AD 816.

The education of adults is an important part of the national education system. The aim is to ensure a high standard of specialized training and professional qualifications. Austrian adults are able to attend university or college courses without necessarily having taken the normal school-leaving examinations. There are many centres for adult education (*Volkshochschulen*) and locally run adult education activities—even in small villages.

Games and Sports

Austria's climate and landscape favour outdoor sports of many kinds. Ski slopes can be reached fairly easily from almost every village and town in the country. In winter-sports events Austrians have often hit the international headlines, and Innsbruck was chosen as the host city for the Winter Olympics in both 1964 and 1976.

Sport as a leisure activity is encouraged, organized and subsidized financially by the Federal Sports Organization, to help keep Austrians fit. Many Austrians—from the very young to some who are quite elderly—indulge in one form or another of sports activity for recreation and enjoyment. There are thousands of local sports clubs. People enjoy archery, athletics, badminton, basketball, billiards, bob-sledding, bowling, boxing, canoeing, climbing, curling, cycling, football, golf, gymnastics, hand-ball, hockey, ice-hockey, ice-skating, sailing, ski-ing, swimming, tobogganing, water polo and water ski-ing—and the list could be much longer.

In recent years many new indoor swimming-pools have been constructed, as well as indoor sports arenas, gymnasiums and skating-rinks. Of course, Austrian competitors are amongst the leading names in the world in the field of alpine ski-ing, and many people who are not experts enjoy ski-ing for pleasure. The ski industry has developed greatly in recent decades. In 1945 Austria had only twelve cable-cars and six ski-lifts. There are now several hundred cable-cars and thousands of chair-lifts and T-bars.

The best ski-ing season in Austria varies with the resort, its position and altitude; most ski-ing takes place between December and March, with January and February as the two main months for winter sports. In high altitudes the

Canoeing – a very popular sport in Austria

Rock-climbing at St. Anton in Tyrol

snow may remain until May. On Kitzsteinhorn (above Kaprun and Zell am See), for example, there is ski-ing all year round.

Ski-jumping is a favourite spectator sport. In addition, many resorts have skating-rinks, curling-rinks, toboggan runs and ski-bob schools. Other sports are popular during the summer. Football is a favourite with both school-children and adults. There are about 250,000 playing members in the football clubs of Austria, making football the country's most popular sport.

Motor racing stars from Austria are frequently in evidence at major international events. Two Austrian circuits, one in Styria and the other in Salzburg Land, are often the venues of international competitions.

Similarly, spectacular cycling competitions are held in the Austrian mountains. The Tour of Austria is one of the toughest amateur races in Europe. It takes competitors over a course of about 1,500 kilometres (over 900 miles), and over the Grossglockner Pass.

Austria's beautiful countryside understandably provides a great attraction for walking and climbing. Climbing and hiking organizations have, between them, a membership of about half a million. There are hundreds of alpine huts where walkers can stay the night; most have a resident warden, at least for the main walking season. Top Austrian climbers have been members of teams which conquered previously unclimbed peaks in the Himalayas and the Andes.

Fishing for trout is popular in numerous mountain streams and lakes. Salmon are found in the larger rivers. Boating on rivers and lakes is also widespread in the summer. Yachting regattas are held on the Wörthersee, on lakes in the Salzkammergut and on Lake Constance. There is also safe sailing on the Neusiedler See where the water is shallow. In winter, when the water is frozen solid and free of snow, ice-yachts are used on this lake.

A sailing regatta on a lake in Upper Austria

The enjoyment of sport and the importance of exercise in the interests of general health are regarded as significant aspects of the nation's sporting activities. There is a nation-wide campaign called FIT-Aktion and the president of Austria is its honorary patron. One of its main functions is to organize large-scale woodland hikes, held annually on 26 October, Austria's National Day.

Customs and Traditions

Traditional dress is still to be seen in most Austrian provinces, although it is usually worn only at festivals or on special occasions. Women wear a cotton skirt, a blouse, a bodice and an embroidered apron. Men wear leather breeches, called *Lederhosen,* bright buttoned waistcoats and hats of black or green felt. The hat may have feathers stuck into it, or brushes of hair from the mountain goat. One of the most colourful local traditions derives from the vineyards. After the late summer grape harvest there are autumn celebrations and the new wine is enjoyed in wine taverns. (Most of the Austrian white wines do not need to be matured.) On these occasions traditional costumes are much in evidence.

Music is often played in the wine taverns—a quartet of musicians is the most usual—perhaps two violins, a guitar and an accordion. There is music in the cafés too. Coffee is a favourite Austrian drink and there are modern cafés in the cities where people can go for a quick coffee. Nevertheless, most people prefer to visit one of the old coffee-houses where many varieties of coffee are on sale—hot, cold, thick, thin, black or gold; coffee with whipped cream, with icecream, with rum—and in many other varieties. Newspapers are provided in these coffee-houses and patrons sit at their leisure reading

78

Open-air cafés in the old part of Innsbruck

the paper, writing letters, chatting or just day-dreaming. *Gemutlichkeit* is a German word that describes the friendly, relaxed and cheery attitude of the Austrians as they go about their business and enjoy their life. Visiting cafés is typical of their unhurried life-style.

In rural areas, festivities—including processions, costumes and bonfires at midsummer—go back to pagan times but are still enjoyed. In many villages the local band plays Strauss waltzes and folk tunes in the square. Dances are held in an open-sided wooden building where the whole village gathers for social functions.

In the autumn, when the cows come down from the hills, they may be decorated with paper flowers and tinsel. A girl sometimes leads the procession and distributes pastries to onlookers. Then, in January, on Twelfth Night, the initials of the Three Wise Men may be written on the doorways of houses to guard the house during the coming year. In parts of the country where these customs and rituals are still practised, the people enjoy them as part of the way of life that has been handed down to them over the centuries.

Whilst traditions still continue, the life of a village or town is continually being altered by the influence of the outside world and by the effects of tourism. Once an area has become

Cows, decorated with flowers, being brought down from the alpine pastures in autumn

popular with tourists there is a likelihood that town-dwellers will soon arrive, looking for weekend homes or permanent homes in the countryside. Tourist areas are often beautiful places and they can normally provide peace and quiet outside the main tourist season. The character of a village is often changed by the tourist invasion. The village of Alpbach in Tyrol is an interesting example of the effects of tourism on a traditional village community. Before 1939 Alpbach was badly-served with roads and the village was largely a self-contained community. In 1945 the first of many conferences was held in Alpbach which, because it was a former mining area, had a number of inns. This event marked the beginning of a new era for the village. Communications were improved, services were extended, new hotels were built and the village—attractive and picturesque—grew in importance as a summer tourist resort. In the late 1950s, winter sports were developed and many villagers became occupied for most of the year with the tourist trade. The valley in which Alpbach is situated began to be settled by professional people from Vienna and other large towns and they built houses for part-time, holiday occupancy. The effect of this encroachment on the countryside is to encourage the growth of an urban outlook; in many respects, the concept of rural life no longer has such a distinctive meaning as in the past.

The Economy

Austria is an industrial nation. In 1980, agriculture and forestry accounted for six per cent of the gross domestic product (the earnings of the country); forty-eight per cent came from mining and power production; and forty-six per cent came from transport, trade, tourism, banking and public services.

Nine per cent of the population is engaged in agriculture. The country is largely self-sufficient in this section of the economy and does not need to import many foodstuffs. Agriculture is now mechanized and efficient. The main product of the forests is pine-wood and this is an important export.

There are plentiful natural resources in Austria—whether of raw materials (iron ore, non-ferrous metals, valuable minerals and timber) or in the supply of power (with such sources of energy as water power, natural gas, oil and lignite). In addition to oil and natural gas deposits, Austria is continually enlarging its hydro-electric potential. But much of the solid fuels and the power need to be imported from other countries.

Tourism brings in money from holiday-makers from abroad and this is beneficial for the economy. Foreign tourists

Folk musicians entertaining tourists in Vienna. (They are wearing traditional *Lederhosen*)

visit Austria in increasing numbers for their holidays; and the money they pay for their stay counts as an export in the economy of the country. Austria's earnings from tourism exceed the income from machinery and vehicle exports. Even with economic difficulties and the recession in Europe, there were almost twenty million tourists in Austria who had short- or long-term holidays in 1982. About five million of these were Austrians on holiday but the others were foreigners.

83

All nine provinces of Austria benefit from tourism but the three most popular (in order) are Tyrol, Salzburg Land and Carinthia; and the next four most popular provinces are Styria, Vorarlberg, Upper Austria and Lower Austria. Vienna is also a favourite city with visitors from abroad.

Many of the holiday-makers who arrive in Austria come from the German Federal Republic (West Germany); they account for about seventy per cent of all foreign tourists. Austria is also popular with tourists from many other countries but particularly with visitors from the Netherlands, the United Kingdom, Belgium, Luxembourg, France, Switzerland, the United States of America, Sweden, Italy and Denmark.

Austria has a varied trade network. She trades with about 150 countries throughout the world. Her central location allows speedy delivery of goods to the east, west, north or south of Europe. Austria is a transit land through which flow the goods of other lands bound for other countries. This is one reason for Austria's good employment record.

Austria was a founder-member of the European Free Trade Association (EFTA) in 1960. The objective of EFTA is to promote economic expansion, to contribute to the development of world trade and to the removal of trade barriers. But membership of EFTA has been less useful to Austria than it might have been, partly because some of her main products are similar to those produced in other member countries. Since 1972 Austria has been partly linked with the European

Economic Community (the Common Market) by a trade agreement. A large proportion of Austrian import and export trade is with the countries of the Common Market.

A substantial part of the economic system of the country is in public ownership. About twenty per cent of Austria's industrial production is organized by nationalized concerns. But, apart from these state concerns and monopolies (such as post, railways, forestry commission, national salt industry, electrical power production and some leading banks), the remainder of the Austrian economy is run by individuals and groups on a private enterprise basis.

Austrians are famous for their hand-made goods, especially costume jewellery. There are also many firms which produce high-quality articles as souvenirs for the tourist market and these form an important part of Austria's exports. Wood-carvers continue the age-old tradition and often carve designs of religious characters. Other souvenirs are made of painted wood or clay. Austrian wickerwork and textiles are also highly prized. Other distinctive products are: Augarten porcelain, produced in Vienna in the rococo style which is highly-ornamental and flowery; decorative enamel-ware, used for trinkets and household articles; petit-point embroidery (a traditional Viennese form of craftsmanship) for handbags, book-covers, etc., most of which are exported.

Important exports from Austria are timber, paper, iron and steel, food, fuel, textiles, metal goods and machinery, chemicals, glassware, aluminium, electric power, women's

Carving religious figures – one of Austria's traditional crafts

fashions, and vehicles—including locomotives, tractors, buses and motor-cycles. The principal imports are machinery, processed goods, fuel and power, raw materials and food. In addition, natural gas and crude oil are pumped to Austria by pipeline. The main nations receiving Austria's exports (and which themselves export goods to Austria in return) are West Germany, Italy, Switzerland and Britain.

86

Living in Austria Today

Most houses in Austria are privately-owned. Many are built of brick or wood. Some have overhanging roofs to help protect the area below from snow. In Tyrol, for instance, there may be a third storey of wood. Tiles and shingles made of wood are used on the roofs and these are often weighed down and protected—by heavy stones or thin metal bars—in windy or exposed positions. Stoves or central heating are needed during the winter. In towns, many people live in flats or apartments instead of in small houses.

Ninety per cent of Austrians are members of the Roman Catholic Church. There is a great variety of church buildings in the country ranging from towering cathedrals to small village churches. These churches often have either a long slender spire or an onion-shaped dome with a short spire on top. The Austrian baroque churches, such as St Stephen's in Salzburg and the Abbey of Melk, have a simple external design but lavish internal decoration, with gilded statues, marble, stucco and detailed frescoes.

On the whole, Austrians are religious people and the local church and its activities form an important part of the life of a community. People are frequently seen praying in church during the day, and (as in other Catholic churches) candles

The Abbey of Melk on the Danube, regarded as one of the finest baroque churches north of the Alps

are lit and placed before the statue of a favourite saint.

About six per cent of the population belong to one of the Protestant denominations.

Virtually all Austrians (about ninety-nine per cent) speak German. But there are small groups of Slav peoples living in clusters in areas of the south and east of the country. There are also Slovenes in the south of Carinthia, and people who speak Croat in Burgenland. In Vienna there is a small group of Czech and Slovak speakers.

Many Austrian meals consist of strongly-flavoured soups,

well-seasoned meat dishes and rich desserts, often in the form of pastries. *Wiener Schnitzel* (which takes its name from Wien— the German name for Vienna) is veal cutlet fried in flour, egg and breadcrumbs and served with salad. Other typical main dishes include beans and bacon in thick soup; diced pork stewed with cabbage; liver dumplings in beef broth; baked fish; roast pork, sauerkraut (pickled cabbage) and dumplings; and mutton boiled with vegetables. But not all Austrians eat rich food. Some are now counting the calories and exercising restraint in their typical daily diet. Breakfast may consist of just a roll and a cup of coffee. Often the main meal of the day is lunch, and only a light snack is eaten in the evening. Goulash (a meat stew with boiled potatoes spiced with paprika sauce) is a very common meal in all parts of Austria. Desserts include *Apfelstrudel* which is a mixture of apple and raisins in a light pastry covering; sponge cakes; shortcakes with a layer of raspberry jam; and richly-filled cakes, of which the most well-known is an iced chocolate cake called *Sachertorte*.

A number of the national dishes of Austria would seem strange to a person who could not read German and they might look like this on a menu in a restaurant:

Rindsuppe mit Fleckerlnudeln (clear soup with noodles)

Lungenstrudelsuppe (beef broth and pastry filled with meat)

Schneenockerln (dumplings of egg-white cooked in milk)

Zwetschenknödel (plums baked in breadcrumbs)

Steirisches Schöpsernes (mutton boiled with vegetables)

Austria in the Modern World

Austria is now a land of contrasts: a prominent European industrial nation but also a land of beautiful mountains, attractive cities, picturesque villages, magnificent castles and green meadows and forests.

The Austrians are a hard-working people. Foodshops in towns are often open for business by 6.30 a.m. Many factories begin the working-day at 7.00 a.m. and office workers are often at work by 8.00 a.m. Co-operation tends to govern industrial relations, with conflicts being settled by negotiation in a spirit of partnership. Rarely are there serious strikes in Austria to upset the national economy. This willingness to compromise is a national trait. It is significant that on two occasions the Nobel Peace Prize has gone to Austrians, and an Austrian has been Secretary-General of the United Nations.

Internationally, Austria has become a meeting-place for the superpowers who come together to discuss world problems. International organizations have also chosen Austria for their headquarters, and major world conferences are held there. The International Atomic Energy Agency (IAEA), the United Nations Industrial Development Organization (UNIDO) and the Organization of Petrol Exporting Countries

The Vienna International Centre, opened in 1979. Since then, Vienna has become – after New York and Geneva – the third focal point of United Nations activity

(OPEC) are based in Vienna. The Vienna International Centre (the third headquarters of the United Nations) was opened in 1979—the same year in which the presidents of the USSR and the USA went to Vienna to sign the SALT II treaty on arms limitation.

The Austrians are proud of their attractive country which has a clean, fresh and tidy appearance. Flowers are grown in gardens and window-boxes; and there are public displays in town centres, as well as hanging-baskets of flowers at many

91

railway stations. Gardens are well looked after and rubbish appears to be spirited away. Even piles of logs for winter fires are stacked very tidily. In travelling around the country, passing village after village, each one picturesque and attractive, set amongst arable fields, meadows or woodland, it is difficult to resist the conclusion that Austria is one enormous and beautiful village.

And yet, it is not a village, it is an independent and important republic. The flag of the Republic of Austria has a red horizontal strip at the top and the bottom and a white strip between. These were the colours of the duchy of Austria as far back as the thirteenth century. The coat-of-arms has an eagle with a crown, holding a hammer and sickle—each representing an important group of Austrians: the hammer for the workers, the sickle for the farmers and the crown for the middle classes and businessmen. There is a broken chain between the eagle's talons and this symbolizes the restoration of Austria's independence in 1945.

Austria has been called the "Island of the Blessed" by the Pope. In the seas of international troubles and conflicts between nations, Austria's permanent neutrality and her determination to safeguard the freedom of each individual give her a relatively stable position within Europe. Austria supports co-operation within Europe and aims to develop friendly relations with all countries.

Index

94

James, Alan

Let's visit Austria.